Dose of Donna

Inspiring Lessons from Everyday Life…

Donna L. Goolkasian

WestBow Press books may be ordered through booksellers or by contacting:

WestBow Press
A Division of Thomas Nelson & Zondervan
1663 Liberty Drive
Bloomington, IN 47403
www.westbowpress.com
844-714-3454

All photographs in this book are from the personal collection of Donna L. Goolkasian.

Interior Image Credit: Photographs by Donna L. Goolkasian and her family and friends.
Cover design credit: Jessica Busby

ISBN: 978-1-6642-9867-5 (hc)
ISBN: 978-1-6642-9862-0 (e)

Library of Congress Control Number: 2023918877

Printed in China.

WestBow Press rev. date: 09/29/2023

WESTBOW
PRESS®
A DIVISION OF THOMAS NELSON
& ZONDERVAN

Dedicated to:
Sarah H. Goolkasian who showed me Real Love
A. Richard Goolkasian who taught me Tough Love
Paul T. Price who provided me True Love

About Dose of Donna

Dose of Donna was conceived in 2000 when I was doing what came naturally—dropping into my co-workers' offices and providing them with laughs, a hug, and most importantly, words of encouragement. Before long, my visits became known as a "Dose of Donna." Because I was passionate about this activity, I wondered over the past 20 years if this could be my full-time job. The thought never left my mind and so with that hope and aspiration, I started providing Doses in writing.

It is my sincere desire that people—those open, willing, and not literal in thinking—will be inspired and encouraged by the insights of my life's journey. Basically, I'm following my mother's advice: persevere through the valley times and celebrate the mountain top experiences. She was my encourager, inspiration, and coach. Could the Dose be yours?

Dose of Donna brings these pages alive in her speaking engagements where she inspires, encourages, and entertains audiences.

www.doseofdonna.com

FOREWORD

Donna and I met in 2010 at a potluck dinner and orientation meeting for a group of nine people traveling to the Philippines. She'd brought a colorful salad. I liked her immediately. I don't know why she and her salad made such a strong impression on me. What I now know is that within minutes of meeting Donna, I had experienced *The Dose*, an authentic, wise, and kind person who graciously engages in conversations that touch people personally, encourage them, and offer up food for thought.

In this collection of essays, The Dose welcomes each reader as an equal on a shared journey of life discovery. Picture a discussion group sitting in a circle, reading one of The Dose's pieces, and relating her words to their own lives. The Dose treats seemingly ordinary subjects with fresh eyes, and her essays lead readers to laugh-out-loud moments, aha moments, and call-to-action moments.

By combining her writing with beautiful photos from her world travels, the Dose takes us on a journey where life lessons play out. No passport needed. Simply read on and savor the lessons The Dose puts forth. They will nourish your soul and put you on the path to better living.

–Patrice K. Jenkins, PhD

February 15, 2023

Acknowledgements with Love

To Zachary Schwartz, first my colleague, then my dear friend who ultimately became the editor for my website and this book. Grateful for the hours you spent to make my voice understandable in print!

To Patrice K. Jenkins, my miracle-working friend who spoke words of wisdom into my soul that catapulted me to create this book. Thank you so very much for helping me make this dream come true!

To the many subscribers who read Dose of Donna on-line. Your engagement was appreciated as it kept me going over all these years!

To my family and friends who gave me that smile and nod as I expressed Dose of Donna … thank you for always listening!

A special thank you to WestBow Press… your patience, guidance and extra patience along the publishing process was so very much appreciated!

CONTENTS

CHAPTER 1

Reach out and touch

Grandma's poodle and Little Dose – circa 1960's

It was a simple touch on the forearm and a complete stranger asked me out on a date! Wow…it was that simple. The Dose later learned that this simple touch conveyed a positive attribute about me that this man found attractive.

There was a time that fellow workers could pat each other on the back, give a colleague a hug or a tap on the shoulder. Not today… there's no "touching" at work; it can only be done with permission.

The Dose believes (and I'm sure it's been well proven) that the touch connects people to others. The touch provides a hidden message – you are worthy, real, and significant. Who doesn't want that?

The hardest people to touch are the unclean, unkempt, and unloved…yet they are the ones that need the human touch most. But here's a thought – could it be they got this way because they were not touched?

In the words of Diana Ross – "Reach out and touch, tell them you care." Didn't someone do that for you?

Five Fingers

deCordova Sculpture
Park and Museum

"I have five fingers... each different, all needed." This was my mother's response to my question "Who's your favorite daughter?" Of course I wanted to be the one, but favoritism was not part of my mother's DNA.

Growing up with such a mother, the Dose follows suit... no one is my favorite sister, favorite friend, or favorite colleague. My eye is quite keen on who's the favorite of whom and I definitely know when I'm favored. It does feel quite nice but when I've been the un-favored one, well, it's downright disheartening.

Favorite, favorable, favored one... it's what I craved as the baby of the family. But now I see the danger of favoritism. It is quite ugly when favoritism is in full sight. Siblings can be affected for life. Employees can become disgruntled.

My mother had it right – each person should be considered distinct and no one should be favored over another. Favoritism is for inanimate objects. So go ahead, enjoy your favorite champagne in your favorite cut-crystal flute while celebrating the specialness of each person in your life.

Ears Wide Open

Somewhere – 2018

My sister had two requests on her 40th birthday – love and listening! It was the listening that captured the Dose's attention.

Who doesn't want to be heard? Paid attention to? Respected when speaking?

In this day and age, politics and religion are not topics to be at the proverbial table. Nope. Too emotional. Too confrontational. Too much. Full Stop - Period!

But what if we really listened?

Though I sometimes try to avoid "challenging" topics, when they come up the Dose has found it beneficial to meet people where they are. When someone has a different opinion than mine, I have at least two options – badger/humiliate/condemn them til death do us part (!) **or** listen with ears wide open.

What does that second option look like? I try to listen, to ask inquisitive (not confrontational) questions to learn more about their viewpoint. What's the harm in that? And I usually find that they reciprocate. Now we both have expressed our points, learning the whys of our differences.

Caught in conversations that are heating you up inside? Chill. Respect the difference and, more importantly, listen fully with ears wide open. Isn't that what you want from others?

My sister had it right – the gift of listening is as priceless as love!

The Generosity Factor

Birthday Card for one year old – 1958

Growing up with relatives who lived through the depression, frugality was a discipline. My uncle watched every penny, yet my aunty would slip little Dose an extra dollar in my birthday card.

That extra dollar may have bought me a trinket but, more importantly, it gave me a memory and a principle that I now live by.

There were days when I'd be like my uncle, carefully calculating the waiter's tip, the bellman's gratuity, and the shampoo girl's thank you. Never giving much thought about generosity, I gave what was deemed appropriate…typically 20%.

And with that 20% tip, the Dose became just an average customer… just like the amount of my tip.

Let's face it, folks in the service industry have a very difficult job for one important reason: most strive to do their best for those they serve! Shouldn't we reciprocate?

In the world of giving, people are known for being cheap or generous.

Be generous to all…the cost may only be that of an extra dollar bill. Ask me how I know…it's been decades since that birthday card, yet I'll never forget my aunt's vs my uncle's gift!

How could less be more?

Darmstadt, Germany –
Thanksgiving 2014

Less is more when there is less stuff to deal with so more time is available.

Less is more when fewer commitments provide us more targeted dedication.

Less is more so we can be less distracted and able to think more of others.

Less is more so that when we receive something, the more we see its value.

Less is more because *more* always wants more and *more* can never be satisfied.

A visit to the Philippines has reinforced this "less is more" principle – those with less are more… more appreciative, more grateful, more thankful, as *less* wants just what *less* needs.

So on this Thanksgiving Day, the Dose is giving thanks for what I take for granted… the ability to help those with less than less.

In the season of giving, how will you be helping others? As it's been said, with your hands open to give, they will be open to receive.

Written on Thanksgiving Day 2010.

Possessing Possessions

320i BMW 1983

Long ago the Dose bought her first car with her own car loan. This was a big deal back in the day. But what was a bigger deal is that I kept that car for 30 years!

This car was a fun-to-drive car – complete with a hand cranked moonroof, lots of chrome, and large car windows... no back-up cameras needed!

Over the years, despite having another car, I also hung onto my first car. Cost was not spared to ensure this old relic of mine continued to serve its purpose... providing me a fun ride on the weekends.

Bottom line: the car was kept in mint condition and, sad to say, "loved" by me.

Eventually the time came when this possession of mine possessed me!

This single gal truly didn't need to have the two cars... and the Dose certainly didn't appreciate the chore of running out to the garage during cold days to check the functioning status of the car battery. As for the cost of the upkeep... I take the fifth.

Things, as nice as they can be with or without a nostalgic or sentimental value, can sometimes just take over... one's time, money, and obsession.

Whatever the material possession that is in your possession, make sure you are the possessor and not the possessed!

Apple, Cherry, Pecan, and...

Bar Harbor, ME – 2015

What's not to like about a pie? There's the crust that consists of butter... lots of butter! The pie filling can range from fruits to pecans. When topped with whipped cream or ice cream, well, then we really do have something delectable.

Enthusiastic about the start of a new job, the Dose was immediately served pie as I took note of the less than optimal accommodations for what I thought I deserved. This pie I did not request nor did I ever crave even a sliver, yet it came with no calories.

The pie? Humble. Yes, the Dose was served humble pie as a reminder to check my pride at the office door.

Not that I had the option to give back the pie or request a different filling... I just needed to accept it and grow from it. And with that, the Dose, with a slightly bowed head, took this pie with grace, as it was better than eating crow!

Humility is an attribute usually thought of as not appealing and a characteristic of a lesser person... one with no self-esteem. But this is quite the contrary. A humble man thinks more often about others and less often about himself.

Humility comes with privileges, as it's often the humbled that serve this pie to the proud!

The Winning "Ticket"

Sahara Desert, Morocco – 2018

Contestants on the Biggest Loser are on the show to lose a tremendous amount of weight. Their goal to drop pounds is accomplished by reducing food consumption and initiating an exercise plan.

And with that, they are in for the surprise of their life… discovering their own stamina!

As the Dose watches these contestants struggling in the gym, screaming at and crying to their trainer, I can't help but empathize. At that time it does seem impossible to do one more push-up, one more sit-up, one more… fill in the blank with anything that looks and feels tortuous.

But at the end of the season, you see the results… results that could never happen without perseverance.

Though I'm not a contestant, this situation the Dose understands. That "one more whatever" looks and feels like the straw that's going to break the back… but it doesn't.

And then, yet another straw is placed on the back and I'm thinking – NO, no more straws – but they keep coming and still the back does not break.

This "camel" just learned what she is made of. Tough lesson. Invaluable lesson.

Perseverance: never easy, often difficult, and guaranteed grand reward.

Stand in Awe

Anywhere post-rain

There he was sitting in a high chair awaiting the song to be over to eat cake. My relative – Richie – was turning one. To celebrate this milestone, balloons were prominently placed in his sight. Richie enjoyed the cake, but it was the big Mylar elephant balloon that captured his attention. A balloon… that's what he was in awe of.

It got the Dose thinking… what I am in awe of these days?

It wasn't too long after this birthday party that I looked at a rainbow in the sky with a different eye. The Dose was in total awe of something she's seen many times. Think about a rainbow. Beautifully colored ribbons in the sky that come out after the rain as a gift with a bow – hence the name – Rainbow! That's the awe – not only the beauty of it but the meaning of the name.

Thanks to a one-year-old child I started looking around with new eyes. Go ahead – look with my eyes… be in awe… life is beautiful!

March 23rd 2008

Paul and me – December 2006

Rewind the tape – it's March 23, 2007 circa 8 AM… I received news that I could barely process – Paul died in his sleep. By the end of the day I faced reality – the man who captured my heart, a treasure I held tightly and patiently waited to share for so very long – my soul mate – was no longer here.

What was I to do…options included escapism…I chose to face this situation head-on. In this choice I knew I needed help – professional help as well as help from those who know me well. So, over the past year I hung out with such people…people who let me fully grieve this monumental loss while gently "holding my hand" so that I could function each day to the best of my abilities.

Now that a year has past, I not only remain in love with my Paul but I show a smile instead of tears when I speak of our beautiful love story. The bonus is my renewed appreciation for those who rallied around me.

Life brings us surprises along the way…some are happy, some are sad. Whatever the surprise, bring in the troops – don't do surprises alone. In good times or bad times, life must be shared.

Written in 2008.

CHAPTER 2

Be Smart... ask!

Me and my purse!

We both wanted the same thing... my purse. Looking at him you wouldn't expect him to want a woman's bag, but then again, what should a mugger look like?

If the Dose had only known that busy main street Baltimore was a scene for a crime, I would have placed my handbag over my shoulder. People were walking to and fro, and cops were directing traffic. Swinging my bag with the rhythm of my walk amongst the crowd of people, it all seemed as safe as the streets of Disney.

Then the war began, the tug of war. A man came up from behind me and attempted to grab my bag. Our wills were equally matched, but our size and strength were not. Once the Dose recognized that, I did the only thing he wouldn't do – I yelled for help!

Asking for help was the one action that kept me from bodily harm, allowing me to keep my purse and showing me the kindness of strangers.

Asking for help isn't a sign of weakness... it's what smart people do when in need!

Number Five

Dad and Mom aka Richard & Sarah – circa 1970's

Honor thy parents. There is nothing in those commandments about friends superseding parents. So why would a parent strive for a friendship with their children?

As a parent, my mom nurtured, cared for, and parented me through the first 29 years of my life. *Parented* is the key word as the Dose looked at Sarah as a mother first and then, later in my life, as a friend. I am grateful that she didn't do for me (or allow me to do) specific things just to be befriended by her little girl.

She didn't need me as a friend and she knew I needed her as a parent. Yet it was the parent in her that made me want her as my friend.

Today, as I observe the parent–child relationship, I often get confused and wonder – who's in charge? Little kids appear to get away with bad behavior despite the presence of a parent. Young adults speak to their folks like they do with their high school buddies. And college kids, well they just ignore their parents altogether… although I'm thinking many do this despite their upbringing.

Parent first – friend later… flip the order and you'll get anything but honor!

This dose is dedicated to my mother, Sarah Helen, on the 25th year anniversary of her death.

Written in 2012.

Leaky Pipes

Waterworks Museum –
Boston, MA 2022

One life lesson my father imparted on my sisters and me was not to build a drain for the drip. If a water pipe is dripping, find and fix the leak, don't just build a drain. Medically speaking it's the equivalent to treating only the symptoms not the source…like prescribing a cough suppressant as effective treatment for lung cancer.

As I think about society, business behaviors, and the like, I see drains being built for the different types of drips. Here's a short list:

- turning up the car radio volume to "drown" out the unusual noise from the car engine
- creating more processes to overcome the lack of accountability from working team members
- buying bigger sized clothes instead of losing weight

Despite my father's advice, in my 20's I built drains for drips. And I will confess, my drains were built to avoid pain and suffering—the consequences of my poor choices.

Building a drain provides ease and comfort …temporarily… but the drip remains and, in the long run, you drown!

Fixing the drip takes blood, sweat, and tears. But in the end, problem solved without regret.

Is there a problem you are dealing with? Take my father's advice: don't build a drain – fix the drip!

Guarantee Return Policy

My kitchen – 2019

Choices are like boomerangs.... results from decisions we make today return to us either constructive or destructive. However, their return may not be as immediate as a tossed boomerang. That's the scary part.

The Dose can provide many personal stories of how this is so true in my life but I'll keep the example simple, straight forward, and non-controversial.

Situation: I was born with flat feet. This deformity (!) required that I wear lace-up shoes during my childhood. Though the Dose dreamed of high heels, I would only be allowed to choose my own shoes when I was older.

Choice: During my 20's, when I was finally old enough to choose my own shoes, the Dose chose to wear high heels at all times.

And so my boomerang was thrown. And thirty years later it came back... as a neuroma, bunion, and bunionette.

Though this choice didn't make me paralyzed, mentally wounded, or affect others, my feet could be in better condition had I chosen differently.

An alcoholic doesn't wake up one day wanting to be addicted to alcohol, but they made many consecutive choices to drink... you know how that boomerang returned.

When you make a decision, project how that boomerang could, should, may return.

Remember, the boomerang **always** returns!

The Low-End Reading Group

Saratoga Springs Public Library – 2022

Third grade. A formative year. A year I remember well... unfortunately for sad reasons. It was the year I was placed in the low-end reading group. The Dose was branded... was it for life?

Through the years, this type of branding has a way of appearing from time to time.

And when it does, my mind has a habit of bringing me back to that third-grade classroom... which then leads to a smile on my face!

You see, though branded as a poor reader, the Dose has persevered through that label with each book I have read. I'm not a slow reader, neither do I lack comprehension of content. My two diplomas tell me so!

Today I find myself in a similar situation. The Dose is the last person on the leaderboard of my spin class. There is an option to opt out of having our names displayed, yet I choose to list my name prominently on that screen.

Why? Well, for starters, I'm on the board... even at the early hour of 5:30am!! I want my name on the board knowing that, like reading a book, the Dose will preserve through.

Ever been misbranded? Rebrand!

Me. Myself. I.

Rome, Italy – 2018

My Dad was a saint. With every school writing assignment, he taught me principles of writing as he corrected the grammatical mistakes and ensured my content was appropriately communicated.

His red ink pen was quick to identify the frequency of my sentences starting with the word "I." My Dad unknowingly foresaw the selfie-generation!

Nothing wrong with selfies, talking about oneself, or starting a sentence with "I." The problem occurs, like ~~most~~, ~~many~~, all problems when it's done in excess or to an extreme.

Selfies can be fun to take, and to share, but do it once too often and it becomes too much!

A one-way dialogue about self… well, that's referred to as a monologue. And unless it's from a comedian, that, too, can lose an audience.

As for starting many sentences with the word "I" – write three consecutive sentences starting with "I," then read them out loud. I rest my case.

Me. Myself. And I. Three words that relate to one person. And though singular, that one person's life connects to others, forming a "we."

Nothing wrong with those three words, yet when there is a "we"… don't forget to acknowledge them before you declare "me," "myself," or "I"!

Lessons from a Colonoscopy

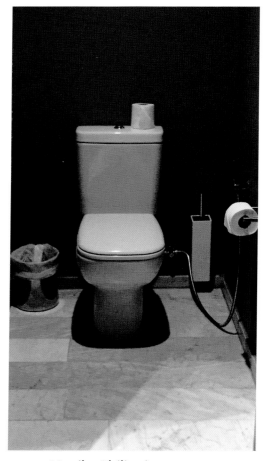

Manila, Philippines – 2010

Colonoscopies don't receive favorable reviews hence the Dose delayed the inevitable... the routine colon cancer screening procedure.

What prompted the Dose to finally complete the test... integrity, walking the talk, peer pressure, and just plain common sense!

Anxiety was my constant companion the day before the test but more so in the hospital's preparation room. This anxiety resulted from the hospital gown adorning my body and the IV running through my vein. You see the Dose was held captive, helplessly sitting in the passenger seat of this expedition... I was neither in charge nor in control; I was totally at the mercy of the doctor and nurse!

And then came the *ah ha moment*... some times we just need to let others lead us, especially when they are the more qualified "drivers." The critical piece is to realize when it's necessary to move out from the driver's seat ... this being one of those times.

Lesson learned from a colonoscopy: some times it's appropriate to put on a Johnny and rely on others and be anxious despite this - it's normal, just like my test result!

Chit Chat Chaos

York, ME – 2012

With one of the largest audience of any American magazine, People magazine does something right. And that 'right' is its content… it's all about people!

People read, hear, and talk about people.

When folks get together, idle chit chat can lead to discussions about people not present. And that conversation may tend to go down some dark path… a path that would appall the person of topic.

Let's face it… we are not immune to such chat. Right or wrong, people are a topic of conversation.

It's a path that the Dose has gone down… despite my mother's advice. Her theory was that when people talk negatively with you about another person, guess who they will be talking about next… YOU!

And she was right… it does happen. Ask me how I know.

Leave the people chit chat to the print in the magazine and go with the adage, "If you don't have anything nice to say about someone, don't say anything!"

Tools of Convenience

New York City – 2016

The Dose was on her way to see the physical therapist. As I read the map to find my way, I thought of all the modern day conveniences, one being GPS. Who doesn't love their GPS, calculator, or spell check? But the question that it got me thinking was, "Are they good for us?"

You see, as I made my way to the physical therapist that day, reading a map and venturing through unknown streets had my brain neurons firing. My brain was working and I know that was a good thing… what the brain was created to do.

No one can argue against the need for GPS, calculators, and spell check, and the Dose agrees that there are times to use these tools of convenience. But she also knows two things: (1) we need to exercise our brains, and (2) these tools are not necessities… you truly can live without them.

I don't want to have to rely on the tools of convenience. An independent, thinking person is attractive. A cashier waiting around for the register to calculate change for her is not.

'Who do you want to be? Think, it does a brain good.

Wishing on a star while flying in the air

Frankfurt Airport – 2013

With a slightly tipped head, the flight attendant asked the Dose – "Any wishes?"

Shocked, stunned, and confused... after a long pause I responded, "Water." Though the Dose had many wishes at that time, I knew to ask for something he could provide.

So with the enjoyment of the refreshing glass of water, my thoughts went to Dose wishes. What is it that I would really wish for if wishes did indeed come true?

Would the Dose want a different life? Should my wish include reversing a decision I made in the past? Do I wish for a change in my appearance, my family members, my IQ?

More interesting question – would the Dose wish be for someone else, include all of society and be more global in nature?

As for these wish thoughts... I do not really want to change my history, what I've been given, or who I am. Why would I? My life's journey is a quality improvement process full of experiences specifically created just for me.

Wishing for world peace and love for all, however, remains on my wish list.

Let the Dose slightly tip her head and ask you "Any wishes?" Wish on!

CHAPTER 3

Will We?

Christmas in Boston – 2021

Where there's a will there's a way. Interesting how the word *will* sounds so much like the word *we'll*.

You know where the Dose is going with this one… my will to achieve sometimes requires a "we'll" to accomplish!

My will to purchase a house required a real estate agent, a mortgage broker, and a group of family and friends to encourage me.

My will to lose weight was supported by the members at weekly Weight Watchers meetings, plus my sister and personal trainer who sat by their computers every Thursday night to read about my weigh in.

My will to persevere during times of trials and tribulations depended upon professional help, people of my same faith, and cheerleaders to root for me along the difficult path.

The Dose believes that where there's a will we just may need the "we'll" to conquer.

Do you have a "we'll" to guide your will to the way?

Do Unto Others

Sahara Desert, Morocco – 2018

Way back when, the Dose went on a date to see Anita Baker and Luther Vandross (God rest his soul) at the old Boston Gardens. Now I'm sure the concert was wonderful, but all can remember about this date was that I walked from the ladies' room to my seat with my rear end exposed!

So what embarrassing things do you see? Toilet paper attached to the heel of a shoe, mascara smudged around an eye, a tag sticking up out of a tee-shirt or sweater, an unzipped pair of pants. My relative is grateful to have me around the dinner table. You see, I provide her the secret signal to pull out the floss when food gets caught in her teeth.

I'm so appreciative when someone points out "irregularities" on me. I only wish that on that date one of the women waiting in the long line to the ladies' room had informed me that my skirt was tucked inside the waistband.

Are you okay walking around with ink on your face, lipstick on your teeth, or having your nose in need of a tissue? I'm thinking not… neither is anyone else. Let's go tell them!

The You of Oz

Stowe, VT – 2013

In The Wizard of Oz, Dorothy's path to a solution was difficult as she encountered lions, tigers, bears, and the wicked witch.

But was it necessary? Apparently not as her answer to how to get home was within her all along.

Who hasn't traveled far and wide – literally and figuratively – to find an answer already tucked inside their very own head and heart?

The Dose doesn't travel any further than the kitchen phone… dialing up everyone in my address book. Yakking it up with friends, seeking ways out of my dilemmas are my common practice.

And now the Dose can see that, many times, my friends prod and probe to the extent that I can spit out my problem's solution buried deep within.

Like Dorothy Gale, I too hold answers, solutions, and a way out… no Wizard needed, just some help from smart friends.

When the tornados of life hit… don't run away. Stick around; keep your feet on the ground, as the answer within will soon be found.

A Priceless Gift

Church of Santa Croce –
Florence, Italy 2018

I am a woman of many words, thoughts, and commentaries.

The good news is I now pause between thought and verbalization in hopes of sparing those around me. This new habit stemmed from being on the receiving end of other people's unprocessed remarks.

In the months of selling my house – a house the Dose just needed to get out from under (figuratively that is) – people reminded me of the bad economy and how houses were not selling at that time.

As my casted foot was healing – the foot being a necessary limb no doubt – the Dose heard all the stories of botched surgeries leaving patients with less than effective feet.

During my unemployment days – in need of a job for many normal reasons – folks informed me of the troubled times we were in and how positions like mine were being cut from the job market.

Although they had good intentions, these informants were telling me what I already knew – the very thoughts that caused me sleepless nights, anxiety, and despair.

Whatever the troubles, problems, or issues people are facing, let's make it a point to give them something they could be struggling to give to themselves: Words of hope – a package that is wrapped up in faith, delivered with love.

Post-op instructions:

> Elevate left foot above heart - ☑
>
> Walk with crutches - ☑
>
> Shower with bag over cast - ☑

These instructions appear totally simple and do-able – all so helpful to heal the incisions of my left foot. How could the Dose not follow Doctor's orders? Yet I needed to follow these directions for a sum total of two months. Eight weeks. Sixty days. 1440 hours… a forever amount of time when only a day has passed.

My *private* thoughts were something like this:

> Day one: not too bad
>
> Day two: not bad
>
> Day three: bad
>
> Day four: brutal
>
> Day five: get this cast off

Day six through Day 60 my mindset changed… for my sake, it had to. The stress of not being able to "do" was doing me in! So I gave myself permission to keep my feet up and just be – being okay to not be all so productive.

My major responsibility was to let my foot heal. Seeing it as a temporary assignment, the Dose put this event into perspective.

Reflective Perspective

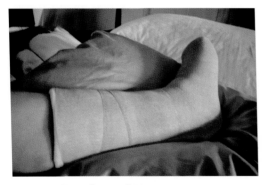

Comfort of Home – 2011

Two months in a cast? No problem. As my mother would have reminded me – it's not a whole lot of time in the scope of one's life.

Reflective Perspective

The Princess & The Pea

London Exhibit – 2010

If you pick up a piece of luggage and it is heavy... without adding contents, do you know what will make it heavier?

Just keep talking about how heavy it is!

Think about it. The more you complain about a situation, the worse the situation becomes. That's why most can relate to the story of the Princess and the Pea.

For those of you who don't know this story, don't feel badly. The Dose learned about this Princess thirty years ago when she was told we were alike. I like the idea of being compared to a princess; the problem is this princess was known for continuously complaining about the small pea under her mattress. Yuck... I used to be just like her. The more I focused on some small irritating thing, like the hissing noise from the radiator, the louder the hissing became.

Even today, I can find myself focusing on something that makes the situation worse than it truly is.

It's time to forget about the pea and be thankful for the mattress.

Short stories mergers and acquisitions

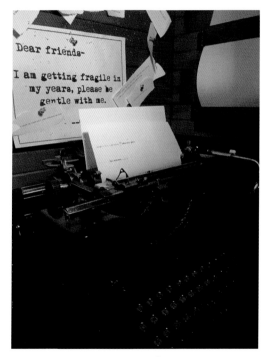

Dear friends-

I am getting fragile in my years, please be gentle with me.

Restaurant Bathroom –
SLC, Utah 2017

The book began with a story about Mary and Dan. In Chapter Two, two new characters were introduced and there was no mention of Mary and Dan. By the time the Dose read through Chapter Three I figured out that this book is no novel – it's a compilation of short stories!

To me, life is a series of short stories that will ultimately read like a novel. Those short stories may appear to end but, unlike the book I'm reading, one life short story builds into the next, culminating as one big epic.

Life is uncertain, incomprehensible situations occur, and when the plot twists we can either accept it and move on, or we can stagnate in despair.

When your life changes, persevere and anticipate a page-turning story with an ending beyond belief. That's what the Dose is going for... After all, a life without plot twists would read like a cheap novel with expected events and a predetermined ending.

Persevere through life and go for the Pulitzer Prize!

The Heart Beat of Life

Fusterlandia – Cuba 2019

Name a song about love and you'll find many love-related associations. Here's a sampling:

Love will keep us together.
Love hurts.
Love is what the world needs now.
Love is a drug.
Love is all we need.

Love... an emotion we tie to the heart... and that's no accident. The heart is a vital organ – pumping "life" though our bodies to keep us alive. Love makes life; Love sustains life.

As there are many types of love relationships – love between family members, friends, and significant others & spouses – so are there many expressions of love. A love relationship is unique between two people and for the most part non-reproducible.

During a New Year's celebration, the partiers – Dose included – were to toast, champagne in hand, our "wish" for others. My wish: for all to know love... the love of a soul mate... the special someone who you just don't want to live without.

That New Year's celebration was the year my Paul passed away... now five years ago. It was Paul who chiseled the cement covering my heart, showed me the love of a mate, and unknowingly got me ready for what is to come in the future.

Got Love? You do have it all... and so will I, once again!

Written in 2012.

Time for Sorbet?

Bar Harbor, ME – 2015

Who doesn't love going to a fancy restaurant? The lovely ambiance, the over-the-top service, the delectable food, and not to mention the chic restrooms with wooden floor-to-ceiling doors on each stall and individual cloth towels. Recently I enjoyed such an experience. Interesting that it was the sorbet served between courses that struck a chord with me. It made me think: should we not have "sorbet" between the "courses" of our lives?

As I think about my journey, I note that the different "courses" of my life – whether it's a change in jobs or the transition between one decade and the next – have often been separated with a "sorbet." I have taken a week vacation when changing jobs. I marked my 30th, 40th, and 50th birthdays by celebrating in "Dose-style." And, when I didn't "sorbet" between significant relationships, the next relationship suffered. These two courses became one and the same…namely, trouble!

Most recently, a trip to Bermuda was the sorbet between my year of grieving and the next year of living without my Paul.

As the restaurant prepares the fancy dish of sorbet to refresh our palates, we need to plan our life sorbet. Is there a transition period coming up in your life? Make certain to enjoy the next course by having sorbet.

Written in 2008.

Ode to Mrs. Jack

Isabella Steward Gardner
Museum – 2021

Mrs. Jack was a socialite who loved art. Her passion was so strong in the arts that she created a palace to share her treasures with the public. This place is none other than the Isabella Stewart Gardner Museum.

Those who have experienced the wonders of this museum can attest to the magnificent works of art that hang on the walls and for the atrium full of flowers and trees, fountains and statues.

Simply breathtaking.

What this woman did was amazing… not just in her ability to design such a palace or her expertise in curating such a collection of fine arts, but in her willingness to share with the world her most prized possessions despite the associated risks.

Though most of us don't have material treasures to share, providing compassion to others is a treasured attribute. Similar to the curated art in a museum, compassion has the ability to bring joy to all who seek it out.

Mrs. Jack didn't need to share her artwork, but she did. With her passion on display, she reached out to touch others. Would you do the same to touch others with your compassion?

CHAPTER 4

Friends and Company

Swati and Me – 2021

Friends... these are the people in your life who share your celebrations, wipe your tears, and pray for the best for you. They are also the people who accept you for who you are and embrace your contribution to their lives.

In the elementary school years, kids termed a certain friend as their best friend. This terminology is so loose that everyone became someone's best friend at one point during those learning years.

Today the Dose is delighted with her collection of friends, friendships, and assorted relationships. Though people have come in and out of my life, with every job I form a friendship that moves on to the next job with me. And there are two faithful friends who have hung out with the Dose for over 20 years!

For the Dose, a true friendship is built on giving, taking, forgiving, and just being... being there for the routine, the good and the bad days, and to encourage as well as admonish. My friends help me grow and I hope I do the same for them.

Here's to friends – true, best, short-term or forever. Whatever kind you are, be the kind you want.

Influencing Partnerships

Prague – 2017

Look at couples who have been married for a long time. Take a closer look. Do you see what I see? Married couples, over time, start looking like each other. Quite fascinating, wouldn't you say?

As I enjoy watching human behavior, starting with my own, the Dose sees something that goes beyond the appearance of these married couples. They mirror each other's behaviors, mannerisms, and choice of spoken words to perfection. Amazing. But not miraculous. It makes total sense... you are who you hang out with.

Being in the corporate world, the Dose can't hold back speaking the lingo of the office. Same holds true with those I keep company with. If the friend I spend the day with enjoys the creative arts, we visit museums or shoot photos. For those who enjoy volunteering... it's off to participate in a worthy cause. As for those who are fitness aficionados... well, the Dose should be connecting with them more often!

My mix of interests does lead to an assortment of friends with mutual influence and alignment of values.

Unfortunately, this was not true in my younger years. Despite my mother's best efforts, the Dose did 'sneak' around with those that persuaded me down paths of, let's just say, no-good.

Who you hang out with does more than keep you company. They have the influence to grow you or distort you... choose wisely!

Glittery Gold

Venice, Italy – 2018

Shakespeare said "all that glitters is not gold." So, what is that glittery façade made out of? Are there really gold-want-to-be's?

Façades can be set up or done unintentionally. The Dose has some interesting ways to set a stage – (1) place vacuum cleaner in living room to give the illusion that I've been cleaning the house and (2) wear exercise clothes and carry around a half-full bottle of water portraying a healthy-life-style Dose!

The unintentional façade is set-up when I'm hiding behind myself. Transparency is the furthest from this behavior…transparency, a behavior I'm known for. The façade sets another stage – starring role – a woman who I am not! This façade can only last for so long. Like all stages, the curtain falls down and hopefully the actors go home as themselves.

Getting close to the glitter provides truth… truth that the glitter may not be gold. Be wary of the glitter that protects their personal space. And should you glitter, make it real… you are a treasure like that of gold!

In the Blink of an Eye

Fusterlandia – Cuba 2019

Twice baked potatoes, double-mint gum, and two shots of whatever. Let's face it – in these cases, one may not suffice. So why give one chance only?

First impressions are memorable. I can remember my first thoughts regarding many people I've met. Author Malcolm Gladwell believes we can make assumptions about people in the blink of an eye. But wait… the Dose has also made some pretty bad first impressions… Am I not redeemable?

Let's face it, we all make blunders, saying the wrong thing, doing the wrong thing… should that permanently determine our branding?

Second chances do happen.

The Dose has sometimes benefited from another shot to display my real self, and I too have extended this grace to others. Giving some people another chance can be more happenstance than deliberate, as long as I keep an open mind, of course!

One blink can give you a perspective, but two blinks may be necessary to confirm or re-evaluate the first impression.

Keep blinking… it just may stimulate others to do the same, giving you your much needed second chance!

Order in the Court

Planet Fitness – anywhere!

The tag line "Judgment Free Zone" adorns the wall of the gym Planet Fitness. The Dose wants not only to wear these words around my neck but also to remember them as I approach other people.

Judging others is an activity that can easily become a sport. I never really saw harm in judging people as the Dose thought of judging as only constructive criticism said out of love. This is how my judgment calls were camouflaged.

Not until I received many such loving, constructive criticisms did the Dose note the danger and pain associated with judgments. In my case, the judges delivered verdicts – whether they were about my behaviors, choices, or use of time and money - based on incomplete and incorrect information. I was guilty without taking the stand or having any other witnesses speak on my behalf. As for the pain – well, some judgment calls were made public and my humiliation ensued.

So the scales finally tipped and the Dose now knows first hand that playing in a virtual courtroom has real, deleterious consequences… most times to the innocent people.

Take off the robe and give up that gavel… trust me, role reversal is only a matter of time.

Excuses Unlimited

East Falmouth, MA – 2019

Excuses, excuses, excuses… we've all got them and we certainly all do use them… especially when all we want to do is say "No."

The other day the Dose got into a conversation about loving dogs… Westies in particular. So the question posed to me was "Why don't you get a dog?" Out came the bag of excuses…I work long hours, I travel, and I just can't do dog care alone. These excuses were like tennis balls – I lobbed one excuse and back came another question. This tennis game went on until I decided to hit an overhead smash by saying, "I may like Westies but I just don't want to get one." Game, set, and match!

Why, why, why do I go on with seemingly rational responses that only invite more questions? The Dose is thinking that the more complex the answer, the longer the conversation. Simple answers like "No or Yes" need to be communicated to end a never-ending match.

And the Dose warns… don't add any more to these two words or you could be back in the game!

You Name It

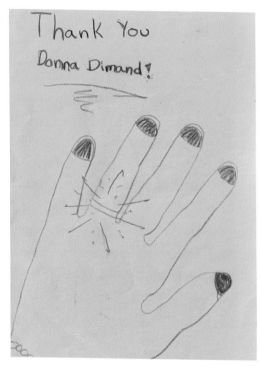

Created by a 9 year old girl

What do Donna Diamond, Aunty Do Da, and Donald have in common? These are names I have been called! Yes, Donald…it's how my Armenia-born grandmother pronounced my name.

Don't get me wrong…I'm pleased with my birth name…but when someone re-names or nicknames me I believe I'm special to that person.

People in my life are special, so when appropriate I dose-i-fy their names. Some are descriptive in nature – FB (aka Jack, my fantasy boss), Laura the exercise girl, and fancy friend Cheryl. One person I "blessed" with three names based upon his attire. When he's dressed in a suit – I refer to him as Henry (his birth name)…dressed in black jeans – he's Hank…dressed in blue jeans – he's Hal (his daily name).

Honey used to be the catch-all nickname for those around me… now I work on more creative names. From the smiles I receive, I believe those with a dose-i-fied name feel special.

Do you have nicknames for those in your life? If not, make them more special…rename them!

The Green-Eyed Monster

York Wild Kingdom – Maine 2006

There were two similar tricycles in the yard: 2-year-old Ray was on one and 3-year-old, Richie, was to ride the other one. Can you guess which one Richie wanted? Yes, the one Ray was riding.

And when they switched, can you guess which one Richie then wanted to ride? Oy vey!

This behavior is not unique to little boys. "I want *theirs*" are three words spoken out loud or inwardly – maybe even in prayers – as an adult. Yes, the Dose can confess to such thoughts but not anymore. What extracted my green eye? Reality!

The green-eyed monster is a robber of time, energy, and joy. Richie wasted more time whining about the bike situation then he spent riding. As for the Dose, I can recall wasted time peering over my neighbor's figurative fence, draining me of the energy to enjoy what was mine and even appreciate what was not mine!

Despite the power of this monster, he is ultimately under your control.

As there are no monsters under the bed… there need not be one in your eye. Let's grow up!

The Value of Words

Fusterlandia – Cuba 2019

Walking out my front door one morning the Dose received a lovely greeting from my neighbor. – "You are the loveliest looking lady in the neighborhood." As nice as this compliment was, it wasn't long after that I heard the same statement by the same man to a different neighbor!

Recently, at a wedding, the Dose was introduced as someone's dearest friend… and, you guessed it, she introduced someone else the same way!

Compliments are wonderful, but they have no value if untrue, insincere, or unsubstantiated.

The Dose has put a practice in place. When making a compliment, I validate the statement. If someone looks nice – I say so and then I specifically call out the attractive component. If someone leads a productive meeting – I say so and then I mention a specific action they executed upon. Basically, the compliment is followed by the answer to the question "How so?"

Compliments – Take them graciously; give them genuinely.

Better vs Worse

Smart vs Smarter

Successful vs Failure

Looking Around, and Around, and Around

deCordova Sculpture
Park and Museum

Comparisons… they are simple to note, effortless to state, easy to make as a habit.

We all make comparisons – my child is better than yours, my spouse is more accomplished than yours, and my house is bigger than yours. Come on; let's not be so foolish. At some point, we can be on the receiving end of such comparisons as well.

Problem – there will always be someone smarter and more successful than me…but that doesn't mean the Dose is a failure. NO! And certainly, I trump someone else in the mind and results departments. But that comparison is just as meaningless.

Solution – keep the comparisons equal by having a common denominator. In other words, the Dose needs to compare myself today with myself from yesterday. I'm the common denominator and time is the only variable when the comparison meter is running.

Stop looking around – start looking within. Take out the yardstick and measure the difference within yourself… it's the true comparison.

CHAPTER 5

Signed with Love

Mommy & Me – Circa 1960's

Today's "dose" is dedicated to my mother, Sarah. She died 24 years ago on February 9th....missing her 63rd Birthday by 11 days.

Sarah Goolkasian, one remarkable woman who remains my role model. She taught me so much about life, love, and living. One significant lesson she demonstrated was to persevere through the valley times and celebrate the mountain-top experiences.

Her way of dealing with the valley times was to put things into perspective, persevere, and know that everything happens for a reason. Sarah was a woman of faith.

My mother also knew that happy times were not always to be everyday events, so when there was a reason to celebrate...she created a party. Her parties ran the gamut – from a buffet of Middle Eastern foods and a houseful of people, to me and her playing cards at the kitchen table with a one-pound bag of black licorice!

Now you know how it is that the Dose can find fun and laugh at the simple things, stay afloat during challenging times, and provide encouragement to others along the way.

The best way I know how to honor my mother is by exemplifying her good qualities...I challenge you do to the same.

Written in 2011.

Tick Tock... Four Years Later

Boston Public Library – 2016

Try a day without time – no schedule, no clocks, no watches, and no looking at the cell phone display. Can you do it? The Dose can't... she's got things to do, people to meet, and places to go. That's the power of time. Accept it.

In some funny way, time has a hold on me and yet the Dose can't seem to get a hold of time. That's the power of time. Honor it.

Time ticks faster when we are enjoying the good times, yet time appears to slow down when we are living through a valley experience. That's the power of time. Deal with it.

Four years ago my sweetheart Paul died unexpectedly. Four years ago the pain was so great that a day without tears was unthinkable. The loss was so tremendous that a sense of peace was inconceivable. Grieving was so exhausting that strength for a new day was unavailable.

And now, four years later this wound of loss has healed over with a beautiful memory of my time with Paul. That's the power of time. Appreciate it.

Time – a friend and a foe yet all for the good to those who respect it.

Written in 2011.

Mirror, mirror, on the wall...

Home Dining Room Mantel – 2022

...how am I perceived by all?

As I look in the mirror, the Dose can't help but see only what I want to see or what I fear to see. The mirror echoes back to my eyes but the image is then filtered through my brain... and there is the start of a possible distortion!

When the brain processes the visual, preconceived notions enter the mix, adding into the reflection and muddling with reality. This holds true for what I see and certainly what others see about me.

And, let's face it, the same thing happens when others look at you. People assess you through their own eyes, microscope, and telescope. It's their view, vision, and interpretation of who you are, regardless of what you say or show. No matter how you rejig your being, you cannot control how others will perceive you.

As for mirrors –they just reflect back – no commentary included.

Mirror, mirror, on the wall... you are the only honest one of all!

Muscle UP!

Watertown Public Library – 2021

The dinner party had started… the table was set, guests had arrived, and burgers were grilling. The Dose was in her glory, visiting friends and meeting new people. Little did I know that at this dinner table I was going to exercise!

My exercise for that night was keeping my mouth shut.

You see, while a lively conversation was happening, one particular couple started a spat – publicly. Their actions activated the Dose mind…should couples publicly argue, claw at and degrade each other? Is this a symptom of an ill-matched couple? And, most importantly - at what point can I step into this conversation? Silence is golden but the Dose likes platinum!

Holding back comments, statements, or any others words within a sentence is an exercise that is as critical as the pumping heart muscle. Making my viewpoint known – in this situation – would have brought me right down to their level of bad behavior.

There is a time to speak and a time to exercise silence. …muscle up!

"Which hand do you pick?"

Butterfly Farm, Aruba – 2009

Both my hands were behind my back, each holding a gift.

The 2-year-old responded with assurance. "Both."

How could the Dose not appreciate such a response …little Richie had it right. Ask for the moon!

As much as I cringe to ask for more, the Dose has learned that this request can pay off. The worst that can happen is hearing the answer "No." I can take the "no" response but what the Dose can't handle is a missed opportunity.

"Right hand" or "Left hand" is a choice imposed on us by others. No reason why we can't add a selection to their lists. It's a simple matter of asking.

"Both" is just waiting to be asked for… unspoken options do exist. It's all a matter of asking – no heavy lifting, no money to exchange, just a shot of confidence and an open mind.

Nourishment for the Noodle

London – 2010

People believe in posting affirmations around their living space – house, car, office. Not a bad idea, as it makes sense to have positive sayings within our eyesight. These affirmations have a way of feeding the mind.

So it is with lyrics.

Music is powerful. It brings us enjoyment, whether humming with the notes, dancing to the beat, or belting out the words to a song. Basically, music has the ability to affect our spirit and ultimately our mood…for good or for bad.

As a lover of Gospel music and my generation's classics – the Beatles, all things Motown, JT* and Carly – I have noted that their soulful lyrics play in my mind long after the song has ended.

You know how that is – we watch the Sound of Music movie and the lyrics to My Favorite Things are on repeat in our heads over the next few days! And it is those instructive lyrics that are feeding our minds.

Feeding your mind with positive affirmations is a good thing that comes in many forms… including the lyrics of the songs we listen to.

Songs. Though you play them… they can unknowingly play you!

*James Taylor

BFF – LOL – BB – BTW

Morocco – 2018

Whatever the abbreviation, acronym, or initials, we all seem to be "short-talking."

As the Dose attempts to get into this type of communication, I'm noting a steep and never-ending learning curve. Though I like typing in short-talk, speaking in this new language slows me down, both as the deliverer and the receiver. TMT (too much thinking)!

Known as the communicator extraordinaire with a specialty in creativity, the Dose knows all too well that each of us has a style, a preference that we embrace. Neither the form, nor the style, nor the manner in which messages are expressed are as critical as the message itself.

And with all that ~~said~~ written, let us not forget our basic form of communication – the Dose's favorite – talking… especially talking to someone in person. This approach seems to be lost in our cyber world, yet it provides more than just words. Eye contact, body language, and facial expressions can never be captured precisely in text or on the phone.

So whether you are short-talking or talking in "long hand," be personable and periodically make your point in person.

A Life Requirement

Salem Willows, MA – 2022

Spring is complete with gardens in full bloom and playgrounds in full motion. Children sliding on the slides, swinging on the swings, and venturing across those monkey bars. And it's the monkey bars that got the Dose thinking!

As a child I would challenge myself on that apparatus, mustering up all of my upper body strength. Letting go of the bar behind me was necessary to bring me forward and across.

Letting go. Two short, simple words glued together to form the most frightening sentence… well maybe this is true only for the Dose.

Letting go. To me this means deleting, eliminating, saying good-bye to what is known, comfortable, and seemingly secure.

My "letting go" experiences include letting go of a previous job in order to enjoy the new job, letting go of a friendship that hampered my personal growth, and – after the death of a love one – letting go of life I had known. Not easy, but necessary to move my life forward.

Hanging on the monkey bars too afraid to let go leaves the child dangling, only looking forward but never moving into the future.

What's holding you back? Let go. Live.

Busy as a Buzzing Bee

Breakfast Buffet – Istanbul 2013

That word – busy – has a certain connotation for the Dose… I can only picture a busy person moving papers from one pile to another. Doesn't seem too exciting to me. Yet, it's frequently the chosen response to the question – "How are you?"

Though I am a busy gal, the Dose sought out to find the best word to describe, well, the word *busy*!

With my amateur market research skills, I tested out three synonyms with one very smart friend.

"Active": implication relates to a sport-minded, exercising person. This is not always the situation with some *busy* people.

"Engaged": though it relates well to what a busy person's life is all about, this word may lead the listening ear down the church aisle when they hear "I am engaged" …even though we mean with life, of course!

"Productive": "I'm quite productive these days…" Here you see someone producing something from their time invested. No mere paper shuffling happening with these folks.

Busy is not a bad word, it just doesn't seem to indicate what we are doing when we say we are *busy*…

Are you just busy or truly productive? Give the answer that reflects well!

Human Splinters

Boston Hospital – 2015

The stairway banister: designed to be helpful, not harmful. But it was. Part of that bacterium-laced banister took up residence as a splinter in the thumb of my friend… leading to hospitalization, surgery, leech therapy, and a new thumb. Yes, that is the power of an object under one's skin!

People can be like splinters. You know the type. The ones who get "under our skin." They have a way of intentionally irritating us. Intentionally annoying us. Their words or actions are like poison – out to infect our very souls by igniting negative emotions.

For the Dose, I find these human splinters not to be messed with. I'm either yanking them out of my life, practicing the fine art of deafening my ears to their nonsense, or simply walking away. Sound cold hearted? Mean? Not all so nice?

My friend ignored that banister splinter and ended up incapacitated for two months.

Like anything that gets under our skin – wood or metal – people who negatively affect us must be addressed immediately or else we too will fall prey to their venom!

Dedicated to John Spuria, who will never ever again underestimate a splinter lodged under his skin.

CHAPTER 6

A Person of Excellence

McGinnis Meadows Ranch –
Libby, Montana 2008

My name is Donna and I am not perfect... neither is the Dose, for that matter!

Hopefully this statement doesn't come as a surprise.

And I expect you realize that you, too, are not perfect.

No human being is perfect.

I am wrong at times. I don't always do the right thing. And I don't always follow the Dose advice I dish out to others.

And with that, the Dose knows that I am right at times, I do the right thing most times, and I follow my own good advice many times.

I'm sure the same holds true for you... no one can be right all the time.

Falling short is inevitable.

Failing happens.

The mark of excellence is getting up and trying again.

It's simple and achievable... it's doing and being one's best.

Move past perfection and go for the gold... be that person of excellence!

Mission: Possible

Balut – Manila, Philippines 2010

Boiled eggs are not difficult to prepare – it's a matter of placing eggs in boiling water for a specified number of minutes. For obvious reasons, it takes longer for eggs to become hard boiled than soft boiled. Key point: It simply takes more time, not more effort.

The same can be said about doing something significant in life... particularly at an older age. As the Dose increases in age and attempts a new adventure, tries a new hobby, or looks for a significant life alteration, I'm often told, "That's too hard to do at your age..." followed by a string of words that only equal discouragement.

The Dose marvels at people over the age of 50 achieving life-long goals of running a marathon, getting a PhD, or changing careers. Their stamina is in-check, their determination is set, and their age is pushed to the side.

And so, I look to the egg placed in boiling water. Whatever the goal, give it some time in a tumultuous situation and it will come out just as desired. Difficult? No. Easy? No. Achievable? Yes, with time, in time... as long as it's realistic!

Missions were not created to be impossible. Think probable!

Short and Sweet

Newbury St – Boston, MA 2015

Typical compliment and associated response:

I love your outfit.	Oh, this old thing?
You look good.	Oh, that's only because I go to the esthetician, stylist, manicurist, blah, blah, blah...
The meal was delicious.	Oh, it was nothing. I bought everything already prepared from the store.

What is it with us… those of us who can't seem to take a compliment? Apparently there needs to be an excuse, rationale, or reason behind something admirable.

Not the Dose – I get the compliment and say "Thank you" without hesitation. People don't want to hear when I got the outfit, who's primping me, or how I prepared the meal… they want to acknowledge and move on.

Don't get me wrong--there was a time that I delivered a dissertation after receiving such compliments. The Dose watched as the compliment giver's eyes glazed over and their thoughts screamed, "Here she goes again."

Regarding the "for modesty's sake" response – saying, "No I don't" in reply to "You look good" – well, that's just a verbal slap in the face!

Hear what is being said… a compliment is a statement, not a question in need of an answer.

An appropriate response is short and sweet: Thank you.

Pete and Repeat were in a boat.
Pete fell out... who was left?

Burano, Italy – 2018

"Tell me that story again." This was toddler Dose's nightly request to her two older sisters.

Oh, yes, I couldn't wait to hear the story of Little Red Riding Hood or The Three Little Pigs. I heard each story night after night but that didn't make a difference, the Dose always needed to hear these stories again and again.

Well, toddler Dose wasn't that far off from adult Dose. As an adult, what the Dose needs to hear, periodically, are unsolicited acknowledgments and recognition.

I may know that I do a good job at work, but only hearing this at the annual performance review isn't going to sustain me throughout the year. And I'd hope a bride and groom hear "I love you" many times after their wedding day.

We all need recognition for a job well done, accolades for the value we bring to others, and acknowledgement of who we are.

Repetition allows the message to penetrate the soul. Applaud, acknowledge, award... then repeat.

Party UP!

Lima, Peru – 2019

Sometimes it just happens… the Dose gets sad and feels like staying in bed. Yes, even the optimists, encouragers, and motivators get the blues. I call these the "valley times."

During the valley times, no amount of prodding to pick myself up is going to help. The Dose just needs to get into a pity party, equipped with a comfortable couch, remote control, and a bag of chips. The deal I have with myself is that the bag of chips needs to be kept small ….no family size allowed! I keep that pity party short.

Whether the blues are triggered by happenings or "just becauses" … valley times do occur in everyone's life. My cure is to indulge in the feeling and, like all parties, set a time to leave. The Dose never over stays her welcome – pity parties included!

So, set yourself up with a "pity party kit" to be prepared when you've stepped in to the valley. Most importantly – don't forget the timer!

Open and Close

Cuba – 2019

The oddest behavior can be observed in an elevator. People walk in, face forward, and stare at the numbers above the door. They rarely look at or speak with other people around them. As you would imagine, the Dose pretty much does the opposite. I walk in, immediately say hello, face sideways, and ask a question or two. As I exit I say goodbye. You can just see the looks I get.

As the Dose analyzes elevator behavior, she's thinking it needs to change. Why? Elevator time provides opportunity. Opportunities open doors. Open doors provide fun. And fun is a good thing.

The Dose is on a mission to shake up the elevator world. It starts with a smile, a sideways-facing stance, and a question. And the conversation can be as simple "Why do we have such elevator etiquette?" This gets the message out and hopefully more people to change elevator behavior.

Try it next time you are riding. In the time it takes before the elevator doors open again, who knows what doors you'll have opened?

Pla(i)n(e) Directions

Bar Harbor, ME – 2015

Frequent flyers can recite the announcement without hesitation – buckle your seat belt, note the exit doors, and, in an emergency, put on your own oxygen mask before you help others.

This last directive may sound counterintuitive but it is far from selfishness.

During my mother's dying days, my aunt delivered the same advice to me. It made sense... how could I take care of my mom if I was without my own "oxygen." She insisted that I sleep and eat right – despite my misperception of no time. Yet it was what the Dose needed for the strength and sound mind to better assist my mother.

To parents, I deliver similar advice: take care of your marriage in order to be better parents. Come on, how can mommy and daddy take care of their children if they're not taking care of each other as husband and wife?

Those flight attendants say more than they realize. When there's a belt – buckle it, wherever you are – know how to exit, and never forget to take care of yourself – first.

Self-care is the first step to caring for others.

Dollars and Sense

Cuba – 2019

It was simple arithmetic, mixed in with growing up during the Great Depression, that gave my parents their smarts about money management.

At an early and appropriate age, my Dad took me to the local savings bank so that I could open up an account. Saving money was critical.

When I got my first credit card, he explained the principles around receiving credit, preaching "Never spend beyond your means… interest is costly!"

As for my mother… well, she taught her daughters to shop the sales. Nice things are wonderful to have especially at a discount!

To this day, the Dose continues to practice these principles. Money for a rainy day… you bet! Can't afford it means I can't have it. And the thrill of the deal is the ultimate high!!

And with all due respect to my parents, the Dose does have some extravagances… but all within reason, all within my means.

In the words of a MasterCard commercial:

The cost of no money in the bank… anxiety.

The cost of creditors mailing, calling, knocking… anguish.

The cost of overpaying… buyer's remorse.

Doing the math… priceless.

Determination was in his eyes – one-year old Henry wanted to walk. Crawling he could do just fine; walking with his hands holding onto Mommy sufficed. But walking solo... Henry just couldn't do it despite his strong will.

What's in your sight?

Arnold Arboretum – Boston, MA 2020

Going from high school to college, changing gears from driving an automatic to a stick shift, and moving from an apartment to a single-family house all seemed so overwhelming for the Dose... just like Henry's situation.

But the Dose has noticed what's critical with any and all personal growth: **focusing on the "prize" and losing sight of peripheral distractions**.

Yes, all personal growth comes with distractions – distortions of reality – and doubts of self. However achievements come with focus, perseverance, and my magic ingredient – encouragement from others.

As for Henry – oh, yes, with Dose as his encourager, he debuted his solo walking skills straight towards the prize.... his mother!

What are you looking to accomplish? Clear the path, bring in the fan club, and never lose sight of the prize – just like Henry, you can do it!

Rest up not on

My Hotel Bed – Morocco 2018

Whether we list them on our resumes, hang up the diplomas, or place the trophies on the mantel, many of us want to "display" our accomplishments. Why not, when we have something to be proud of? Trouble starts, however, when we rely on our historical successes to achieve in our current affairs. Laurels are not foot stools!

Having had a handful of jobs, the Dose quickly learned that I needed to re-prove myself with each new boss. Telling them my gold-star history at my previous jobs was meaningless, ineffective, and downright foolish. These new bosses needed to see and experience the effects of the Dose in real life action…words on a resume are just that.

It's good to have success stories and it's wonderful to have achievements, accomplishments, awards, and the like. Though the past can't be pasted into the future, it sure can motivate us to create more.

Resting on our laurels is as supportive as standing on quick sand. In life, it's best to rest up not on as you're going to need energy to prove yourself over and over and over and over!

CHAPTER 7

Caught Yellow-turning-Red Handed

Dresden, Germany – 2015

He said it was red... I'm sure it was yellow. Regardless of what the Dose had to say about the situation, I received a $100 traffic fine. $100 for the ticket and more dollars tacked onto my car insurance for the next three years.

As I ventured on in my car, over the next 24 hours the Dose couldn't help but observe other drivers – two specific drivers that clearly went through a red light... clearly, no questions, no doubt about it. However there was no police officer there to stop them, charge them, and humiliate them. Not fair.

After a few days of digesting my "guilty verdict," I paid the fine.

And I recognized that not all injustices are captured – mine included. As the Dose continued to process my driving style, I became grateful for the times authorities didn't see when I was "slightly" over the speed limit or was too distracted to let a pedestrian cross the street. If I were caught for every traffic violation, well, let's just say the Dose would be without a license!

Fair? Unjust? Whatever the assessment, if we all do the right things in life, our hands would be untainted. Right on...

The Crimes of Life

Alcatraz Federal Penitentiary – 2017

Wife is found dead... prime suspect: the husband.

So why do husbands who kill their wives think they are not going to get caught?

Is undergoing the process of being arrested, prosecuted, and jailed truly worth killing your spouse?

The real question is: why do we do things that ultimately get us in trouble?

Child Dose got herself into so much trouble she quickly learned how to lie her way through those toddler-plus years. Teenage Dose worked on doing wrong but privately. Close-to-mature Dose considered herself a white-collar criminal... always seeming to be right, thanks to credible alibis, as she did wrong.

Whatever the wrongdoing – done privately or otherwise – I got caught. My no-no's were uncovered by parents, friends, and by the cop in my head (aka my conscious).

Mature Dose now knows that running and hiding from wrongdoings is exhausting work. Between the worry of being caught and the energy necessary to squish down my feelings of guilt... well one just can't enjoy their bad behavior. That momentary pleasure is ultimately outweighed by associated detrimental tribulations!

The detectives always find the murder, the sin is always exposed, and the consequence is never avoided.

Whether in your mind or in your town, there's a prison that awaits you... Stop misbehaving!

As Dark is to Light

Mirabell Gardens –
Salzburg, Austria 2017

As dark is to light, silence is to noise.

Silence. Lack of noise – a form of darkness.

To the Dose, it's as close to death for me here on earth. Sure, I like quietness when falling and staying asleep, but silence when my mind is screaming? No. I don't like the silence when I'm wrestling with my thoughts. The Dose prefers a noisy distraction!

In a world of lights and sounds, silence is not always welcomed. Maybe some of us don't like silence because then we have only our thoughts to hear… thoughts that need to be reckoned with or acted upon.

But, even though I may not like it, silence is the one thing the Dose needs during such times. Sorting through my thoughts is a one-talking-person job. A listener may be required… but not one who talks over or through my mind's voice.

The sound of silence – as said so eloquently by Simon and Garfunkel – is where I find a whisper of wisdom.

In these stress-filled times, meditation is tops on the 'to-destress' list.

Meditation is code for welcome the silence and listen for the whisper!

'Til death do us part'

Mt Auburn Cemetery –
Cambridge, MA

Whenever I hear about a person dying or of a death, the Dose ponders the question "What would that person do differently if they could relive their life?"

If the person were a workaholic – would they have wished they relaxed and vacationed more? If the person died alone – would they have wished they connected more to society and people? If the person had a large family – would they have wished they did more (or possibly less) for each member?

Of course I would never know the answer to these questions but it leads me to think – what can I learn from this person's life and now their death?

On the day after Steve Jobs' death – the Dose is remembering to live out my passion. Fortunate for most of us, Mr. Jobs exercised his passion. This is what I hope for for the Dose.

We've all heard that life is short – the question is, knowing that, what are you going to do differently? If you know that answer – time is ticking - wait no longer!

Written in 2011.

Road Trip of the Mind

Havana, Cuba – 2019

Sometime it just happens… the inspiration isn't present, the mind goes blank, and nothing can be written. Happens to all writers – Dose included!

It seemed the harder I tried to put words on paper, the fewer letters I typed. My editor was waiting for the next dose. Readers were asking if I was ever to write again. And my website designer was thinking, "After all this work I did, she doesn't post?"

Self ~~inflicted~~ created pressure and deadlines ultimately led to the stalling of my repertoire of work.

It seems that the more pressure to do something, the more it doesn't or just can't happen. Happens to all people –right?

So what was the Dose to do? The one thing every writer does: write! They write. They write every single day. They write a few words, or a few paragraphs. Every. Single. Day.

Sometimes the solutions are so simple, it's all a matter of common sense and persistence.

Roadblocks happen, but it doesn't mean the road trip is over. Keep the engine running… you'll eventually get there!

Bubbles on the Beach

York, ME – 2018

The Dose loves all facets of summer – taking time off, hosting BBQs, and blowing soap bubbles. Little did I know that the simple bubble wand of my childhood years is not only **not** in vogue, it's considered boring… even to two-year old Matt!

As I dipped the wand in the bottle of liquid soap and blew through the wand's circle, Matt looked at me confused and definitely uninterested. Apparently the battery operated bubble maker at his house produced more bubbles, bigger than my little wand could muster.

Have the simple things in life been taken over by costly inventions?

Back in the lazy days of summer, I used to make doll clothes, create art with chalk, and play jump rope and ball. Despite the limits back then, the Dose grew up learning how to be innovative, creative, and resourceful.

Whatever latest glitziest toy is calling your name, buyers beware: your right brain may fall asleep.

Don't let your mind go on vacation - go "retro" play… no serious cash required!

Bye Buy!

London – known for news, money, and law. This city is also associated with the monarchy, high tea, and Harrods. And with all that London has to offer tourists, the top question asked upon my return was, "What did you buy?"

Buy? Wait, the Dose needs to tell you about the experience… not the shopping!

My father's mantra was "go travel… go learn." He was right. Traveling is an education and with every trip I've taken the Dose has come back with more than a shopping bag.

Seeing how the "foreigners" live, learning the history of the location, or enjoying local activities makes the visit more special than any shopping trip. Over the years of going places, I find myself talking about the experiences, thumbing through the photos and brochures, and preparing meals related to my various travels. Trips have certainly given me knowledge and good conversation.

As for shopping…oh, yes, the Dose usually brings back a unique purchase reflecting the visit.

Go travel… go learn – experiencing the things and food you can't back home all to be captured in pictures, a journal, and that much assumed memento!

Ghost in My Machine

Boston, MA – Summer 2022

The iPhone is complete with an intelligent personal assistant named Siri. Upon your command, Siri will set the alarm, send a text, or dial a number. She also verbally responds when you ask a question or make a statement… responses include "I live to service," "I aim to please," and my all-time favorite, "I'm incapable of worry."

Incapable of worry… Siri, the Dose so wants this attribute! Imagine never worrying about, well, you name it. As I play that imagine game, my shoulders stop shrugging, and my body relaxes. With worries pushed aside, the Dose can't help but think better thoughts – more productive thoughts – definitely happier thoughts.

Over the decades of having something to worry about pretty much every day of my life, I'm taking on Siri's being. Though I'm not wired like her, I can manually reprogram my thought center when heading down the path of worry. And for times when I can't, the Dose can have Siri set the timer, reminding me to limit my worry time so that I can continue being human but not considered a worrywart.

Siri, unlike you, I am capable of worrying, but thanks to you I won't let worry make me incapable of living!

Situation Comedy

Portland, ME – 2014

Sometimes the Dose finds herself in unconventional circumstances... often thinking, "How did I end up here?" Here are some examples of what I'm talking about: I've been in a morgue watching an autopsy, in the front seat of a fire engine on the way to a call, and at the Brown family Thanksgiving table knowing only one person – Mrs. Brown. How does the Dose get into such interesting situations?

Let me explain the way I got myself into the morgue, the fire engine, and the Brown Family house. It's called adventure... risk taking... opened mindedness. If the situation isn't going to cause the Dose harm, she goes. From these situations I have an even greater appreciation for the human body, the men who fight fires, and the Brown family, even Mrs. Brown's in-laws!

Spur of the moment activities need momentary thought, but some can't be missed for what's waiting on the other side. So, go join in life's adventures... and remember, many of the unplanned ones are the best!

Simple Comfort

Charles Bridge – Prague 2018

There is a two-letter word that provides the Dose comfort…"we." The significance of "we" became apparent thanks to a person you would least expect…a real estate agent!

Between 1993 and 1995 I worked with Cathy, my real estate agent, as I changed houses. It was two long years of showing my house and bidding on others. This whole process was extremely emotionally draining, but the word "we" provided me unexpected comfort. Cathy would call me up to inform me that "we" didn't win the bid …"we" didn't have anyone at the open house.

Being single and dealing with life challenges can be scary … Cathy figuratively stepped into the situation with me with such a seemingly insignificant gesture.

How do you provide comfort for others? It can be as simple as a two-letter word.

CHAPTER 8

Focus Time

Burano, Italy – 2018

There are many words that describe the Dose… a multi-tasker is one of them. When I've got the dishwasher running, the feather duster dusting, and a phone conversation going on at the same time, I'm in my glory. Quite pathetic but true!

What is sadder for me is that the Dose now must end this type of behavior… a behavior that I've always proudly stated as one of my qualifications for employment opportunities. But it needs to happen before I burn down my house.

You see, the other day while I was at work, I asked my property manager to run to my house and shut my windows as a severe rainstorm was impending. To his surprise, I had left eggs boiling on the stove. That morning I had been rushing around, multi-tasking away, getting myself ready for work. And, apparently, cooking eggs.

To my amazement, nothing catastrophic occurred… the only evidence was particles of eggs shells on the floor, a burnt pot, and very hard-boiled yolks.

I'm uncertain if multi-tasking is innate or a reflection of my environment… whatever it is, I'm going to start enjoying each task without being distracted by another!

What's distracting you? Don't be the cause of your own distraction, or your own destruction!

DotCom(munity)

· · · · · ·

· · · · · ·

· · · · · ·

· · · · · ·

· · · · · ·

These dots mean absolutely nothing until they are connected. With the stroke of a pen, the dots can be connected to form a picture – one that that could never be without the participation of other dots.

Some days the Dose feels just like one of these dots – unconnected and quite frankly, without meaning. It's on those days that I notice my lack of connectivity with others even though people are all around me. This "dot" didn't realize that if another "dot" didn't reach out, I needed to. Key word: need.

I need people. I need them to help me… to socialize and share life with. And let's not be fooled – the Dose needs people to love and be loved by… don't you?

Despite Streisand's lyrics, I'm not a "luckiest people." The Dose is just like you and everyone else… **all** people need people.

One dot need not connect to all, but by reaching out and connecting with one, which further connects to the next, here in forms the basis for humanity.

"Connect the Dots" – it's not just a game… it's living.

Heart Holes

deCordova Sculpture
Park and Museum

It was a hot, humid afternoon in July and the man at Starbucks was ordering hot chocolate. If this request didn't get the Dose's attention nothing was going to.

The dialogue began.

"Interesting order," I stated.

His response... "Something has to fill in the potholes of my heart."

Just as potholes in the road are visible corrosions from the elements, I imagine that, in the human heart, potholes are corrosions from the emotions of life. And, like potholes in the road, heart holes certainly cause damage if you don't see them nor address them.

My heart potholes most likely come from the hurts others unconsciously inflicted on me, my own self-doubts, and the cravings for those deceased loved ones. I don't want my heart holes to have an ill effect on my life or those around me so I need to "spot and fill." Spot the hole and fill it in with the makings of my heart... love!

So, seeing that chocolate is a symbol of love, I guess the man was on the right track on that hot and humid summer day.

Do a self-heart exam... take note of the potholes and fill them in with love – love of yourself and love of others around you.

Location. Location. Location.

Bangkok, Thailand – 2013

Square peg in a round hole.
Fish out of water.
Misfit.
Odd duck.

Call it what you will, feeling out of place is downright uncomfortable. Unfortunately, it took the Dose a long time to figure out that when I'm displaced, there's nothing wrong with the place or with me… it's the combination of the two that's not right.

In the past, when faced with those situations, I would do all that I could to assimilate and integrate. The Dose wanted to fit in because if I didn't, well, then there must be something wrong with me.

The square peg belongs in a square hole.
Fish belong in water.
Misfit and odd duck are labels.

We can choose to either accept or reject names people call us. We can also choose to find the place we belong. There's nothing wrong with the square peg or the round hole … each was designed for specific purposes.

When I find myself as a square peg sitting in a round hole, the Dose now has choices – leave or offer what this "peg" can provide in any shape.

Wherever you are, whoever you are…find your place or shine where you are!

A – MUSE – ing

The Highline – NYC 2017

Years ago, the Dose participated in a creative artists' workshop. Being amongst other creative folks, I frequently heard the question asked, "What's your muse?"

So it was appropriate for the Dose to ask her artist sister, "What's your muse?"

The conversation quickly turned into a comedic banter with silly questions such as "Are muses just amusers?" and "Can someone be an amusing muse?"

As fun as this lighthearted discussion was, the Dose had to muse about the muse.

What is my source of inspiration to write my life lessons? How does my muse show up at the time of need? Could I be a muse for someone else?

It wasn't long after pondering such thoughts that the Dose recognized a reciprocal relationship between muses. Those who glean from my life lessons inspire me to write, and I inspire them forward to be the finest version of themselves.

As amusing as this may sound, everyone needs a muse to help create their best life. Who is yours?

'Going to the Dogs'

Lisbon Airport – Portugal 2018

Ivan Pavlov, a man known for his dogs... the dogs that simply responded to a ringing bell rather than applying critical thinking.

As a child, learning about Pavlov's dogs, I couldn't help but think, "How sad... these dogs are not smart enough to process the situation, and hence they are fooled."

The disturbing truth is that, at times, the Dose can be a Pavlov dog, too. The stimulus? Technology <u>calling</u> (pun intended) makes me react and respond to my smartphone without thinking and takes me down a path that most times is un<u>called</u> for.

Unlike Ivan's dogs' actions, this mindless behavior has been accepted by society. I've seen this device take over people's being – at business meetings, at dinner tables, and even at the movies! Recently, the Dose couldn't help but ask my niece "What text is so critical to respond to as we sing Happy Birthday to you?"

It's not the device that puts us in a trance... it's us being "Pavloved!"

Let us keep a leash on ourselves by thinking for ourselves.

Wait a Minute, Hour, Day, Month, …

Prague – 2017

Red – stop; Green – go; Yellow – wait.

Love the green… dread the red. As for that virtual pause button – the yellow light is an apparent ~~annoyance nuisance~~ sign of torture!

Waiting was the name of the game in my childhood. My sisters and I had to wait for a certain age before we could stay up to watch Ed Sullivan on TV, get our ears pierced, or date boys. Though the light was yellow, we knew the signal to go was only a matter of ~~time~~ age.

Into adulthood, waiting doesn't seem as easy since guarantees of what we want are never provided. And at times, it seems that we are **forever** stuck at the yellow light of life.

The Dose has been there – stuck, paused, and waiting… and waiting… and waiting. With no signal to move, it's tempting to forge ahead and it's easier to stop and turn around. Yet both moves are fraught with risk. The road lights of life will change as they always do. Red will prevent danger; green will provide more than a heart's delight… kind of like the reward for being so very patient!

Waiting: it's not for the faint at heart – it's for those with a heart that doesn't faint.

Delete Fast Forward

Bedrock Gardens – Lee, NH 2016

There are many difficult life situations – being unemployed, getting a divorce, and suffering from a chronic illness – just to name a few. One of the hardest is watching a dying loved one.

The Dose learned this first hand when my mother died from a terminal brain tumor. Though this experience was over 20 years ago, a key lesson has never left my mind: Stay in the moment - don't miss it by looking into the future.

This key lesson began on Christmas Day 1985. The Dose spent much of this day focused on the "what if." What if this was to be my mother's last Christmas? I just couldn't help myself, as the future without Mom was soon to be a reality. And with that thought, I frequently ran into the bathroom for some cry time, totally missing much of that day with Mom.

Well, Christmas Day 1985 was not my mother's last Christmas; that happened in 1986. And there was my life lesson. I had missed what could have been a wonderful Christmas.

It's true, watching a dying love one is difficult, but missing moments with them is regrettable.

The future will come soon enough… Stay in the moment.

Written in 2010.

Conviction Friction

Bedrock Gardens – Lee, NH 2016

"Hurry up and agree with her or she'll keep at you until you do!"

Occasionally I hear these words spoken from the past referring to yours truly – the Dose. Fact is, it was true… I just couldn't give up the "fight" until the listening ear agreed.

We all encounter times when conversations go down disagreeing paths. Each party's point of view seems reasonable, acceptable, why-not-able. And why shouldn't it be? People have passion in their positions. It's called conviction and without conviction, we'd be like vanilla ice cream… neutral and quite boring.

The Dose has discovered two options for such impasses in conversation – avoidance and acknowledgement.

Avoid the conversation altogether. Why bring up discussion points that only get folks hostile… though it is entertaining when **all** parties agree to discuss and not argue their viewpoint.

Alternatively, acknowledge. When you have either placed your foot in mouth or you don't want to continue an undesirable conversation – stop the madness and agree to disagree!

Convictions are no reason to give up conversations and conversations are no reason to give up your convictions. Stay true to yourself – just remember others are doing the same.

Walk the Tightrope

Cliffs in Maine – 2015

Nik Wallenda–daredevil, trapeze artist, the man who went across Niagara Falls on a tightrope to inspire others to live their dreams. Since the age of six, this was his dream, a big one no one can argue. And decades later he made it happen.

As a child, having such a dream would only be considered as such–a dream. Imagine Nik telling his friends even five years ago of such a dream? The Dose can hear the responses: "Who do you think you are to accomplish such a feat?" "What are you thinking, it's never been done before?" "Where are you going to get the funds?" "When? How?" and the last comment, said with an explicit laugh, giggle, or chuckle, "Good luck with that!"

Thank you, Mr. Wallenda, for following your heart's desire, for doing the necessary training, and most importantly for not listening to the naysayers. You have inspired not only me but hopefully many others as well.

Thanks to Nik, the Dose has a new saying–"walk the tightrope." Translation: dare to live your dreams.

CHAPTER 9

Human Statues

Bangkok, Thailand – 2013

Statues at museums and those in public places are set up high to foster an upward gaze.

Looking up to those carved sculptures can provide a sense of awe as we study the work of art--and probably a sense of admiration for the person captured in stone.

We too can be considered a statue, a human statue otherwise known as a role model, for those who choose to look up and emulate the you in them.

In the business world, there are leaders who mentor those new in their careers. That's role modeling for a cause.

But what about role-models for living life well?

No surprise that my mother was my role model. I watched her make a home, engage in volunteer activities, start a professional career later in life, and most importantly, live out her faith. All those accomplishments were done with grace and excellence.

Be aware, others could be on the lookout for their role model, which may be you!

Act well, make decisions wisely, and smile... you never know if a "mini you" will soon be in the making!

Lights – Color – Action

Christmas Mantel – 2022

Blue and White

Red and Green

Silver and Gold

These colors can all represent one thing – December! Yes, this is the month that is bright with color and shine from all the glitter and lights.

Interesting that during this one month a metamorphosis occurs. Think about it:

> our hearts are open to give to those without;

> people are intent on visiting family and friends, seemingly trying to get along better than at any other time of the year;

> spirits tend to be lifted as we reflect on the season.

As a society we appear to be more generous with goods and time. We think more about those without. Everyone seems to be united.

Though the religious holidays ignite these colors, celebrations, and traditions, need their essence end after December? When celebrating the meaning of the season – whatever it is for you – consider a yearlong after-party. There will always be people in need, family and friends who want your company, and spirits, like mine, that need a lift… all year round.

This is a wonderful time of the year; it need not end. May the spirit be with you - always!

Kindness is a currency

Prague – 2017

The worth of a dollar bill is different in each country, yet the value of kindness is the same worldwide. It's a unique currency that is freely given yet never depletes.

To me, a person who is kind is different than a person who is nice. Nice people do seemingly nice things... kind people do what is right for the other person.

To me, the act of kindness has a spirit of generosity... and one of consideration. Like love, it places the other person before themselves.

To me, practicing random acts of kindness cannot be forced. It needs to come naturally, intuitively, and from the heart.

To me, kindness was not meant to be hoarded... it's the currency that is intended to be disbursed.

To me, I see one act of kindness sparking the next... as kindness begets kindness.

To me, kindness comforts the soul and brings joy to the spirit...to both the giver and receiver.

Therefore, to me, the more kindness that is expended... the richer the kind person becomes.

The Dose has kindness to spend... do you?

Be Kind.

Because My Mother Said

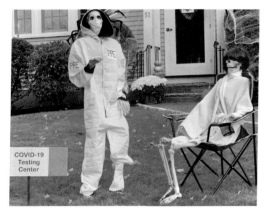

My Neighborhood – 2020

She told me time after time, "Donna, don't ever forget, there are more good people on this earth than bad."

Who's the she? My mother, who unfortunately died in 1987.

Every now and again, this thought comes back to the Dose. I see acts of good, but the seemingly bad behaviors appear to overpower the news.

During this COVID-19 pandemic, we see the good in others come through like a knight in shining armor racing through the wilderness. Doctors and nurses have stepped in to comfort the dying for those family members who cannot be with their loved ones. Strangers have sponsored meals for hospital workers and tirelessly made face masks for those in need. Apartment dwellers are intentional about looking after the elderly in their building... and company manufacturing plants have been transformed to build the much-needed ventilators.

These acts of kindness have superseded those that felt the need to hoard toilet paper and hand sanitizers.

Yes, there are people who commit evil. There always have been and there always will be.

So, do my Mother's words still ring true today? Yes. Not only because she said so, but because good overpowers evil and spurs on more good!

Be Good. Do Good.

Written in 2020.

Passion: 'Today'

Acadia National Park – Maine 2015

The Westin Hotel employees in Maine have name badges complete with a display of their passion.

Michael the concierge listed his passion as travel, but it was the passion of the General Manager Bruce that caught the eyes of the Dose. Bruce's passion? Today!

And there I had my point to ponder for the two-hour drive home. Is the Dose passionate about today… every day?

I'm thinking Bruce sees each 'today' as an unknown adventure ride in the bigger Disney World called life--each today having thrills that have never been experienced before, all awaiting his engagement and enthusiasm.

But is today a repeat of yesterday? The same old grind… repeated five days a week? I'm thinking not. Each day may appear typical, but like Bruce, when the Dose approaches 'today' with passion, each day is new adventure. I never know what the day will bring… a new acquaintance, an opportunity, or a challenge that stretches my mind or faith.

This adventure ride, unlike those in Orlando, cannot be repeated. Each 'today' is brand new and with that comes new possibilities.

All due to a simple name badge, the Dose has embraced the passion called 'today.' Care to join me?

The Heart

deCordova Sculpture
Park and Museum

Who decided that love comes from the heart? Could it be because, ultimately, the heart keeps us alive? We were created by love, for love…that only a beating heart can give.

Love comes in many flavors – true, real, and tough, just to name a few.

The Dose has experienced such love. Real love from my mother. Tough love from my father. And true love from my sweetheart Paul.

All these forms of love boiled down to one commonality – the love they showed me focused on my best interest. These three people in my life cared, taught, and developed me until their untimely deaths.

The self-less love from my parents modeled kindness and self-care. My relationship with Paul gave me the opportunity to put love to the test… putting his needs before mine and trusting he would do the same.

Love is a word that is best described by its action. In the rawest form, love reflects putting others ahead of ourselves.

Can you imagine a world where everyone loved each other in such a manner? Ultimately, we would all get our needs meet in the most wonderful of ways!

Do. Love.

Why? Why? Why?

Morocco – 2018

Sounds like the start of a dose from a 2 year old! But it's not... it's the Dose pondering the "whys" of life. And, sad to say, I've got theories but no answers to the infamous question "Why do bad things happen to good people?"

Back in 2003, the company employing me was running out of funds. Every month an employee or two was being let go. My turn for the pink slip was in August of that year.

Bad. Bad. Bad.

Flash-forward four months later, my career was catapulted beyond belief when I was hired by a company that laid the foundation for my professional success.

Good. Good. Good.

Bad happens... I just need to make good out it. That I can do, well, at some point after the whining, grieving, temper tantrum is over.

After pondering this infamous question, the Dose has re-worded the question to what I believe is truth – "Why do *perceivably* bad things happen to good people?" There has never been a situation that I have not experienced the good out of bad – it's all been a matter of time.

Two in One

Bar Harbor, ME – 2015

Bumper stickers are interesting reading, especially when sitting in traffic.

Some are funny. Some reflect the car owner. Yet there are others that are thought provoking… just like this one:

What if your dreams are where your fears lie?

Interesting thought that the Dose enjoys pondering. And I must confess that many dreams have led me to face my fears.

As a little girl I wanted to be an actress… to be on stage with a spotlight and microphone. With that dream came stage fright. Though I never got to be in the performing arts, my college work included a course on how to deliver presentations to healthcare professionals… not exactly an easy crowd! While the dream of being on stage was not (possibly yet) fulfilled, the fear was conquered… a dream in and of itself.

And now I see that whatever dream I have, there are frightening obstacles that can either cause the Dose to dismiss the dream or ultimately persevere and conquer.

Most dreams come to fruition through motivation and drive… unless they are dreamt through a "pipe!"

If your dream awaits you in your field of fear… well, now, wouldn't entering that land be a small price to pay for such a triumph?

"Life" after "Death"

Havana, Cuba – 2019

In the world of antibiotics, there's a phenomenon referred to as the "post-antibiotic effect." It means exactly what it says – there is an effect from the antibiotic that continues even after the drug is gone. Pretty good deal – take the drug and its effects outlast its time in the body!

Wouldn't it be nice if other things had a post-effect. For example a one-dollar bill would provide future transactions without the need for payment or a small bit of food would produce a feeling of satiation over a very extended period of time.

The Dose has experienced a post-effect. Though my sweetheart, Paul, died three years ago today, his love remains within my heart. His thinking, ways, and style have influenced me during his life and now during his post-life. In other words, Paul "continues" in my life despite his absence.

This post-effect was unexpected, yet one that we are all capable of giving to others. A woman's perfume scent lingers, spoken words are remembered, and images remain in the mind's eye.

Provide your post-effect – make it positive, make it indelible!

Written in 2010.

No Response Needed

deCordova Sculpture
Park and Museum

To: Listening Ear
From: Dose
Re: Today

Dear Listening Ear,

What a bad day I had today. I should have known that it was going to be such a day when I overslept, had a flat tire driving into work, and my computer crashed while crafting an important document.

Blah, blah, blah...

Thanks for listening.

-donna

It's easy to read this memo and start figuring out solutions around alarm clocks, tire pressures, and hard drives... most of us are helpful, helping people and wanting to lend a helping hand. Nothing wrong with that. Or is there?

The point of ~~complaining~~ venting is to release tension, calm the spirit, and renew the soul. Some days the Dose just needs to rant. I'm not always looking for a solution.

Just think if this memo had been sent to "Answer Man." The steam vented out would have only found its way back to suffocate the innocent! Venting is a one-way action that should **never** boomerang back in any form or shape.

On the receiving end of a venting session? Turn on the hearing aid and listen up!

CHAPTER 10

Aprons not required

Cooking in my kitchen – 2012

Top chefs and master bakers have sacred recipes that have been tested to perfection. Each ingredient is measured with accuracy and carefully added ensuring the most pleasurable culinary experience.

Life has a tried and true recipe too. We have our basic ingredients – eating, sleeping, working – those standard components that are at the core of an adult's life. The spices of life are those events & people that provide the flavor and uniqueness.

Like any good cook, the Dose looks for the distinction in each recipe that produces the piece de résistance. For me, life's special ingredient would be none other than HUMOR!

Humor does for me what good medicine does for an ailing body. Humor brings the Dose through difficult situations. It provides relaxation in times of struggles… it can cause a belly laugh, bring people to tears, and yet it can make me pause and forget my concerns.

The secret to adding humor in the recipe of life is to know the appropriate quantity. Some days can accept a cup full of laughter while other days can only handle a pinch of levity.

Be a mindful cook – taste the scene and add the fitting amount of wit.

The Value of Free

Outdoor Exercise Park – Istanbul 2013

In our country, we have the opportunity to enjoy things and experiences, all seemingly for free!

We have beautiful parks, beaches, and mountains to enjoy. Cities and towns provide their residents with baseball fields, playgrounds, and outdoor skating rinks.

Shops provide women with beauty samples. And Costco generously serves up samples of tasty morsels!

Nothing inherently wrong with free. But is free valued?

My favorite "free" is the public library. Many old town and city libraries are within beautiful buildings rich in architecture. They house some historical books and documents and provide a quiet space to read, browse, and nap!

For the Dose, I appreciate the books, movies, and music... all available for the asking. And seemingly free!

The value of my rentals was specifically realized on two occasions – the time the Dose had to pay full price to replace the library book I dropped in the ocean (!) and, more recently, the time when the library slip specifically noted the value of the books I had checked out!

Free isn't really free... there is a cost. And though you may not be the one paying the price... honor those who do by appreciating its value.

The Language of Languages

Teddy Bear Tea – Gloucester, MA 2016

Though my mother was born in the States, she spoke fluent Armenian… making the conversation between her and my grandmother very foreign to me.

When I was younger, I had no interest in learning a second language – English was enough for the Dose to comprehend and grasp!

Regardless of one's linguistic nature, the language of love is probably the easiest to learn.

As love is a verb, it needs no words… yet it can be conveyed in the distinctive language that the recipient understands and desires.

There are many languages of love, which speak differently… conveying affirmation, serving others, giving gifts, providing one-on-one time, and/or hugging tightly.

My love language leans towards one-on-one time topped off with a big hug (virtually acceptable) from those I love. Material gifts, affirmations, and driving Miss Donna, though appreciated, are not my love speak. Those who know and love me know this too!

Tell someone you love that you know them by speaking *their* love language. But first remember to investigate their speak!

Say What?

Flower Delivery – 2020

Have you ever been in a situation where you just didn't know what to say?

The Dose has been in many, and I've witnessed things that probably shouldn't have been spoken. Like the woman who asked my dying mother, "If they diagnosed you sooner, would your prognosis be better?"

And let me not be remiss in disclosing that I, too, have said seemingly foolish things.

As I analyze those times of foolishness, it was typically when I truly didn't know what to say.

What do you say to a person with the diagnosis of cancer?

If you are like the Dose, coming to the rescue with uplifting words of encouragement *seems* appropriate. Yet that is the last thing the hurting party wants to hear. The same holds true for questions asked out of curiosity. Duh!

I've done the research… these folks desire kind acts from understanding hearts. It's these acts that provide the unspoken words – I'm here for you – in the form of a hug, a held hand, or a listening ear.

Say what? Say nothing… Just do!

Good Grief

A Cemetery – 2015

Grieving is a process. A process with steps to take in order to come to terms with a death.

It's hard work. It's not fun. Yet nothing worthwhile is ever easy.

Grieving is often associated with death of a loved one. Yet, grief also comes when there is a loss of a circumstance, a bodily function, or a dream, just to name a few.

Regardless of the situation, the Dose has learned that grieving doesn't erase the loss from my mind… but it does aid in loosening the grip in order to move forward.

How did I learn this? By not grieving. I thought I could escape the pain by jumping over the loss. But when the next loss showed up… well, then the Dose was faced with a double dose of grieving! Case in point: When my father died 11 years after my mother – I had to grieve them both.

As for other losses… those require grieving too! People with chronic disease are challenged as they lose a form of functionality. That loss requires the grieving process as well… all to move forward by accepting the hard reality.

Loss is not good… but grieving well is.

Out of Order

You know where! – San Francisco 2017

No lie, I once stopped in at a Starbucks only to note the sign: Out of coffee.

Then there was the day I walked into a bank to make an in-person withdrawal, and the teller informed me they didn't have money. No lying here either.

A coffee shop without coffee and a bank without cash. Odd... but not considered so for the Dose.

You see, I'm associated with expectations as well... expectations to inspire, encourage, or downright entertain and/or engage others.

However, the Dose, too, can be fresh out of whatever I need to serve up.

It happens. Shops run out of beans, banks don't receive the proper supply of funds to shell out, and sometimes the Dose is, well, basically exhausted. All three need to be replenished!

So, like the coffee shop and the bank, going back to the well is what I need. My source to refuel is found in rest.

This downtime, quiet time, alone time, allows me to regroup, renew, and refresh... all to restock my supply in order to dole it out to others!

Starbucks, the bank, the Dose--and you for that matter--can only provide what is stored within.

Take time to fill up so that you can be ready to serve up!

The Life Cycle of an Apology

Boston Symphony Hall – 2019

When I was growing up, mother required many things from the Dose… doing chores, practicing table manners and, my least favorite, saying, "I'm sorry" when necessary. That last activity took much coaching from Mom. Today, my conscience illuminates my Mother's teachings… there's a clear cycle of life with the act of apologizing.

Opening Act

> The act of apologizing starts with me even if I'm not 100% to blame.

Act 2

> Once my conscience has identified the target – the person negatively affected by the Dose – the confession is made. Whether I convey, "I'm sorry" or "Forgive me," these short communication points provide a verbal hug or handshake.

Grand Finale

> The moment those words are sincerely stated, the act of apologizing comes back to me as my conscience provides the Dose more tranquility than any drug could provide… quite the addiction-provoking action!

Apologizing does come full circle…as does not apologizing. The only difference is the final act isn't so grand.

Take center stage – fess up – then bow.

Mind-SET

Cuba – 2019

We set the table in preparation for a meal.

We set a clock to display the time.

We set the oven temperature in order to bake.

Settings are important for our expectations as well. Having proper expectations of an event and, more importantly, of others is critical. Without setting realistic expectations, disappointment is guaranteed.

Non-dog lovers aren't going to enjoy your new puppy.

People who don't enjoy sweets aren't going to appreciate your home-baked cake.

A blind person can't tell you that you look good.

As the Dose listens to the frustrations of others, I've taken note that they are often expecting something that will never happen. Folks who know the Dose know well that I'm not quite sure how to interact with youngsters. So expecting me to babysit, or be totally engaged in children's play would be a bit... well, ridiculous. You would be let down and I'd be clueless of the significance of your disappointment.

Some expectations are obvious, others need to be unveiled... whatever the case, set the mind and proceed accordingly!

Cards, Cake, and Candles

L espalier Restaurant –
Boston, MA 2017

Birthdays – love them or hate them. It's your choice.

The anniversary of one's birth needs to be considered a special day. This is the day that you were welcomed into the world… the day your mother labored selflessly to aid in this wonderful event.

Though some birthdays may not be as happy as others, my special day is always marked for recognition, even if just for me. A day off from work is typically in order, as is cake!

And now that the Dose is turning a very big age, one that many women hide from, I'm welcoming the next decade with delight. The alternative is to be miserable and the Dose doesn't have time to be miserable… my life now is truly short!

In the saying Happy Birthday, the "Happy" is intentional. It is a happy day. Ask any new mother with a newborn. She maybe tired but she is most certainly happy!

A birth-day anniversary is just that – a marker of your entrance into life… sure beats the alternative!

Happy Birthday!

Written in 2017.

The Best Year of My Life...

San Fran Airport – January 2017

...thus far!

Play the word association game with the word "resolution" and usually the following phrases are front of mind: dieting, exercising, and quit (fill-in-the-blank)-ing.

Resolutions—most of us have made them along the way, and most of us have ditched them on the side of the road by springtime.

This past year, the Dose made an unusual resolution. One that was sustained every single month.

As 2017 marked the year of a very big birthday, the Dose just had to make this year different from the rest... one that would be memorable, be exciting, and catapult me into the next decade with no regrets.

And with that, I lived this past year as if it were my last. Though it sounds somewhat morbid, it was the year I fully lived!

Every month I secured something to look forward to—an event, a vacation, or a self-improvement activity. In addition, the Dose stopped overthinking and made several decisions to complete home-related transformations.

The Dose was fully engaged by intentionally taking the first steps towards participating in what life had to offer. This behavior circled around the question "What will I say I did during this very special year?"

Don't waste time... what do you want to say about 2018?

Written December 31, 2017.

About the Author

Dose of Donna was conceived in the year 2000, in a small-office setting, where Donna L. Goolkasian would provide co-workers with laughs, a hug, and--most importantly--words of inspiration and encouragement for the day.

Years later, Donna now provides inspiration and encouragement through her life lessons in writing... this is your "Dose" of Donna.